SONGBOOK

CONTENTS

SONGS

What fun is in store for you today! This RECORDER FUN™ SONGBOOK will have you playing the recorder quickly and easily while you learn to play your favorite songs from THE DISNEY COLLECTION SONGBOOK.

ISBN 0-7935-9370-0

Wonderland Music Company, Inc. and Walt Disney Music Company

DISTRIBUTED BY

HAL•LEONARD®
CORPORATION

7777 W. BLUEMOUND RD. P.O. BOX 13819 MILWAUKEE, WI 53213

Visit Hal Leonard Online at
www.halleonard.com

GETTING STARTED

HOLDING THE RECORDER

Here is how to hold the recorder. The mouthpiece rests on your lower lip, just like a drinking straw, with only a little of it actually going inside your mouth. Be sure that all of the finger holes line up on the front of the recorder as shown in the picture.

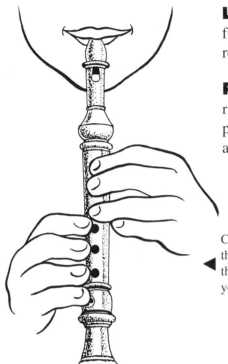

LEFT HAND — The first three fingers of your left hand (the little finger is not used) play the *top* three holes on the front of the recorder. The thumb of your left hand plays the hole on the back.

RIGHT HAND — The *bottom* four holes are played by your right-hand fingers. There is no hole for your right-hand thumb to play so it can help hold the recorder steady while the other fingers are busy playing.

◄ Cover the top three holes with your left-hand fingers and the bottom four holes with your right-hand fingers. The thumb of your left hand covers the hole in the back of your recorder.

MAKING A SOUND

To make a sound on the recorder blow gently into the small opening at the top of the mouthpiece. You can change this sound by covering different holes with your thumb and fingers. For example, when you cover all of the thumb and finger holes you will get a low, quiet sound. When only one or two holes are covered the sound will be higher and much louder.

Here are some tips for getting the best possible sound out of your recorder:

Always blow gently into the mouthpiece — Breathe in and then gently blow into the mouthpiece as if you were sighing or using a straw to blow out a candle. Remember, always blow gently.

Leaks cause squeaks — Play the holes using the pads of your fingers and thumb (not the tips). Press against each hole firmly so that it is completely covered and no air can sneak out. Even a tiny leak of air will change a beautiful tone into a sudden squeak!

Use your tongue to start each tone — Place your tongue against the roof of your mouth just behind your front teeth and start each tone that you play by tonguing the syllable "du" or "too" as you blow gently into the recorder.

PLAYING A TONE

Musical sounds are called *tones*. Every tone has a letter name. *Finger charts* are used to show you exactly which holes should be covered in order to play a particular tone. Each circle on these charts represents one of the holes on your recorder. The thumb hole is represented by the circle to the left of the recorder in the chart.

● means that you should cover that hole.

○ means that that hole should not be covered but left open.

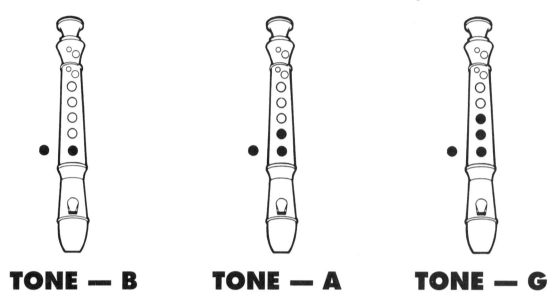

TONE — B   **TONE — A**   **TONE — G**

Use these three tones to play "Mary Had A Little Lamb:"

MARY HAD A LITTLE LAMB

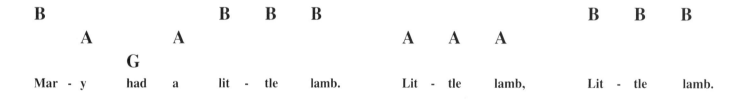

B				B	B	B					B	B	B
	A		A					A	A	A			
		G											
Mar - y	had	a	lit - tle	lamb.			Lit - tle	lamb,		Lit - tle	lamb.

B				B	B	B	B			B		
	A		A					A	A		A	
		G										G
Mar - y	had	a	lit - tle	lamb	whose	fleece	was	white	as	snow.

READING MUSIC

Musical notes are an easy way to see everything that you need to know in order to play a song on your recorder:

How high or low — Notes are written on five lines that are called a *staff*. The higher a note is written on the staff the higher it will sound.

How long or short — The color of a note (black or white) tells you if it should be played short or long. The black notes in "Mary Had A Little Lamb" are all one beat long (*quarter notes*). The first three white notes in this song are two beats long (*half notes*) and the last note is four beats long (*whole note*).

How the beats are grouped — The two numbers at the beginning of the song (4/4) are called a *time signature*. This time signature tells you that the *beats* in this song are grouped in fours: **1** 2 3 4 **1** 2 3 4 etc. To help you see this grouping, *bar lines* are drawn across the staff to mark each *measure* of four beats. A *double bar* is used to mark the end of the song.

Now here is how "Mary Had A Little Lamb" looks when it is written in musical notes:

MARY HAD A LITTLE LAMB

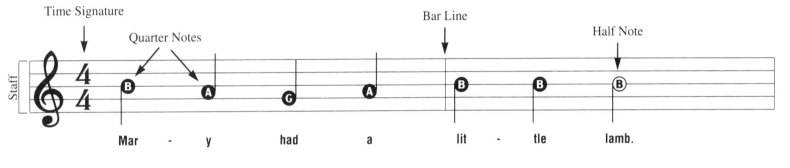

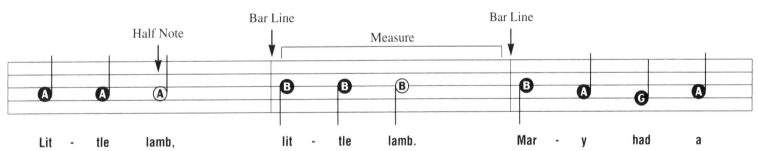

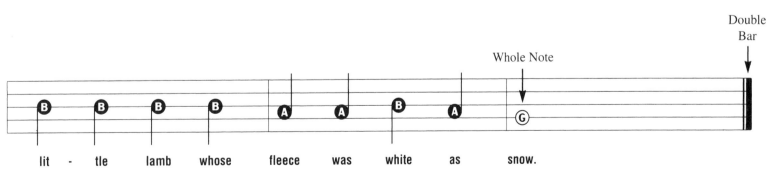

TWO NEW TONES

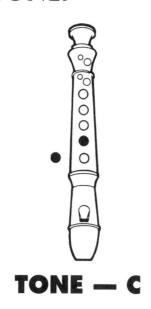

TONE — C

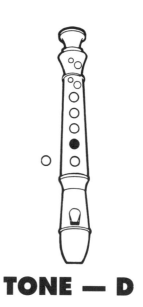

TONE — D

AURA LEE

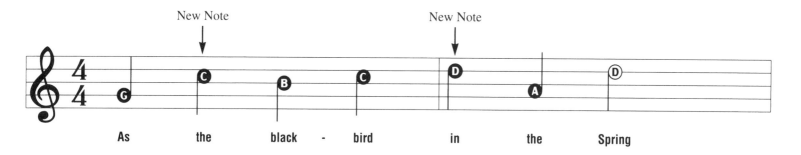

New Note

New Note

As the black - bird in the Spring

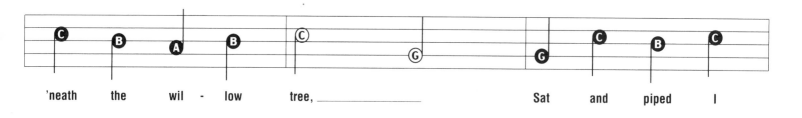

'neath the wil - low tree, _____ Sat and piped I

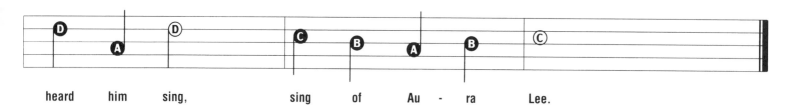

heard him sing, sing of Au - ra Lee.

USING YOUR RIGHT HAND

"Twinkle, Twinkle Little Star" uses the tone E. As you can see from the fingering chart, you will use three fingers of your left hand and two fingers of your right to play this tone. The thumb hole is only half filled in (◑). This means that you should "pinch" the hole with your thumb so that only a small part of the hole is left open. Pinching is done by bending your thumb so that the thumbnail points directly into the recorder leaving the top of the thumb hole open.

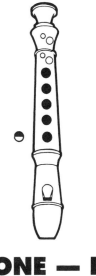

TONE — E

TWINKLE, TWINKLE LITTLE STAR

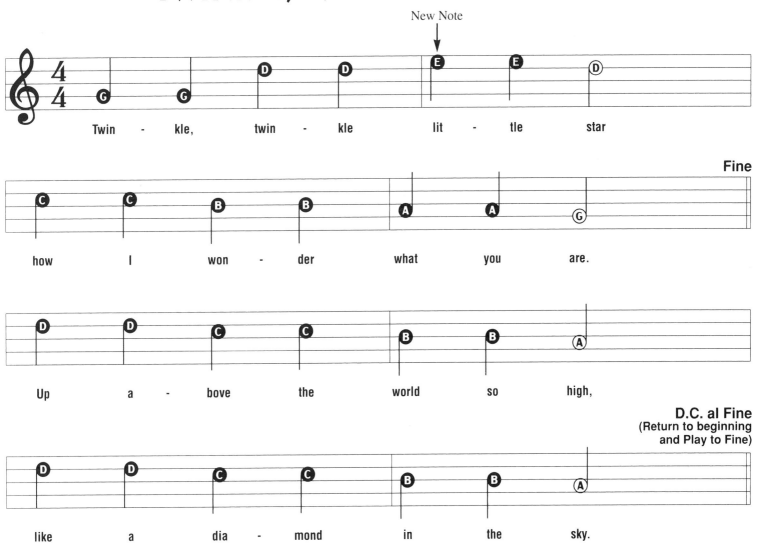

Copyright © 1992 by HAL LEONARD PUBLISHING CORPORATION
International Copyright Secured   All Rights Reserved

NOTES AND RESTS

In addition to notes that are one, two or four beats long, other values are possible. Also, *rests* are used to indicate when you should *not* play a tone but be silent. The chart on page 7 will help you identify the different notes and rests that are used in this book.

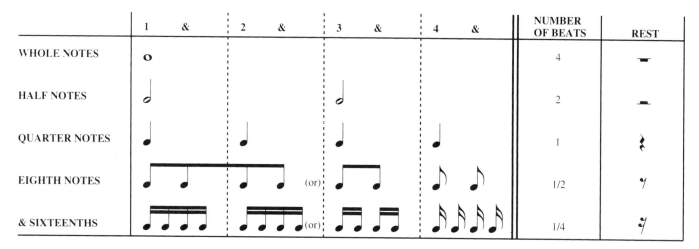

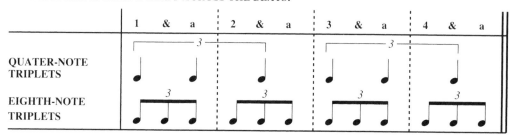

THIS OLD MAN

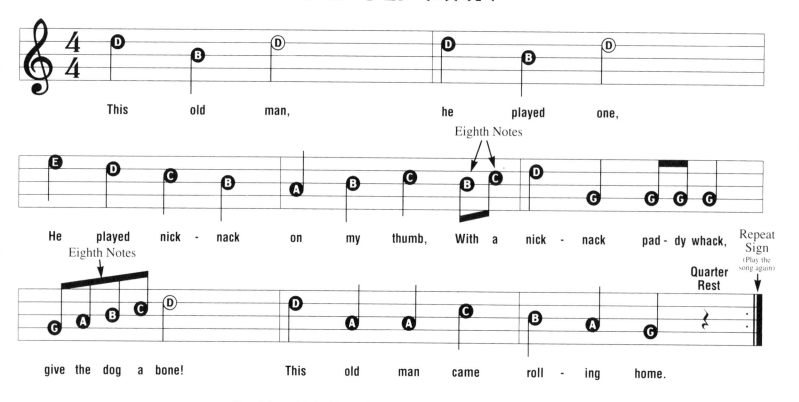

FINGERING CHART

Some tones have two names (C♯/D♭, D♯/E♭). These are called enharmonics. Even though enharmonic notes look different, they will sound the same.

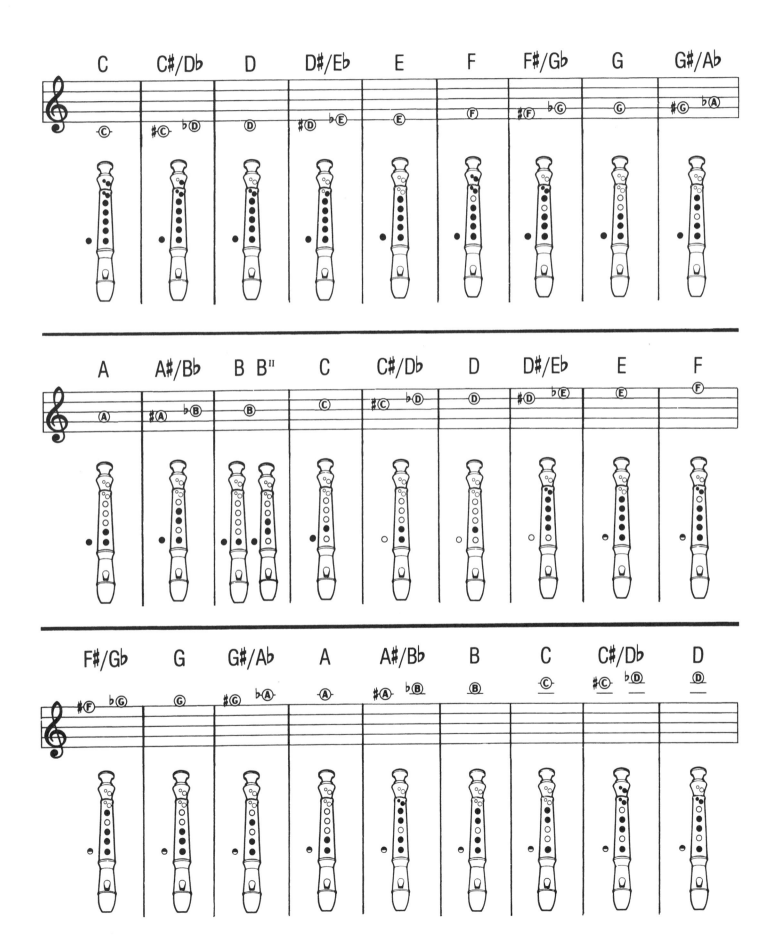

Can You Feel The Love Tonight
from Walt Disney Pictures' THE LION KING

Music by Elton John
Lyrics by Tim Rice

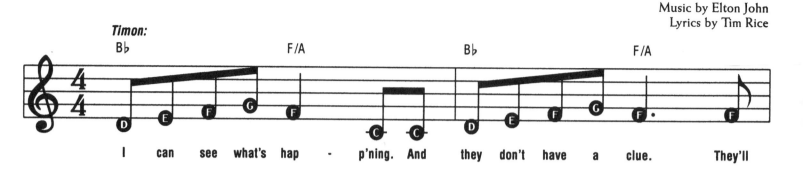

Timon:

I can see what's hap - p'ning. And they don't have a clue. They'll

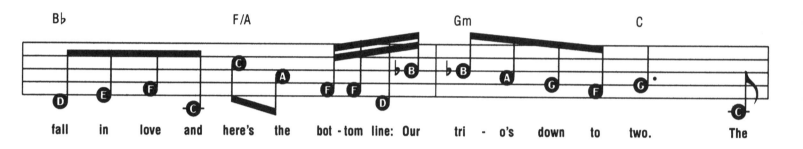

fall in love and here's the bot - tom line: Our tri - o's down to two. The

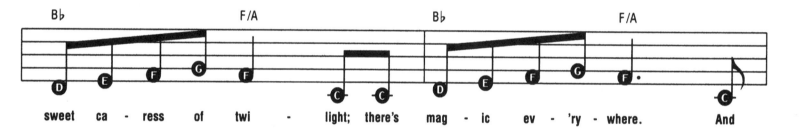

sweet ca - ress of twi - light; there's mag - ic ev - 'ry - where. And

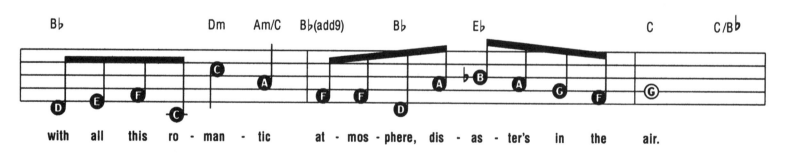

with all this ro - man - tic at - mos - phere, dis - as - ter's in the air.

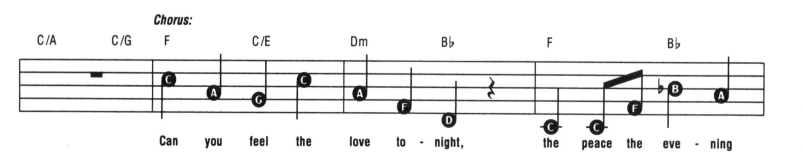

Chorus:

Can you feel the love to - night, the peace the eve - ning

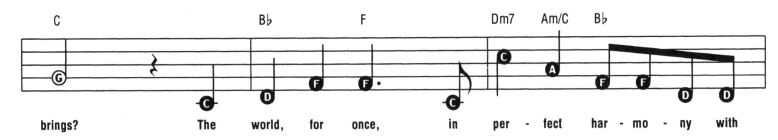

brings?   The   world,   for once,   in per - fect har - mo - ny with

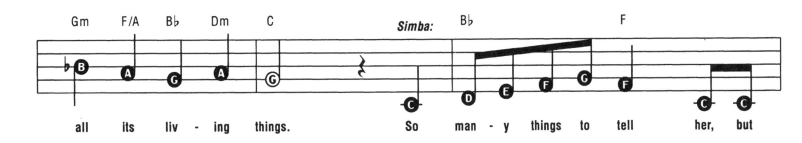

all   its   liv - ing things.   So   man - y things to tell   her,   but

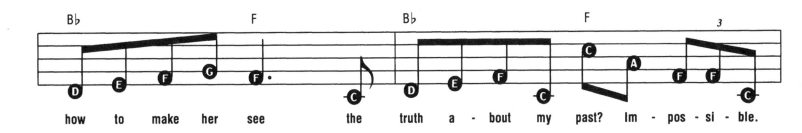

how   to make her   see   the truth a - bout   my   past?   Im - pos - si - ble.

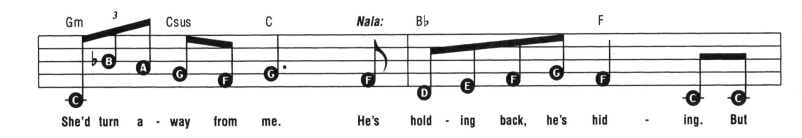

She'd turn a - way from me.   He's hold - ing back, he's hid -   ing.   But

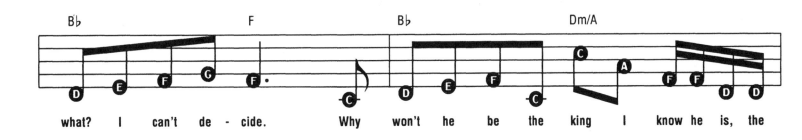

what?   I   can't de - cide.   Why won't he be the king I know he is, the

Chorus:

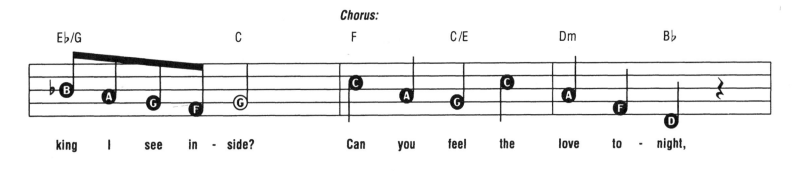

king   I   see in - side?   Can   you   feel   the   love   to - night,

11

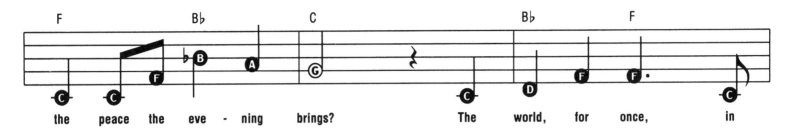

the peace the eve-ning brings? The world, for once, in

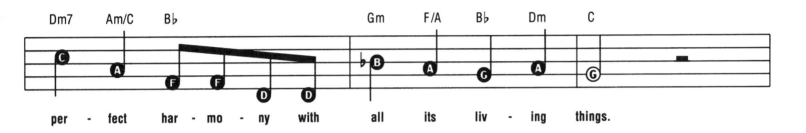

per - fect har - mo - ny with all its liv - ing things.

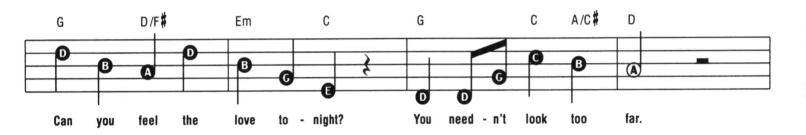

Can you feel the love to - night? You need - n't look too far.

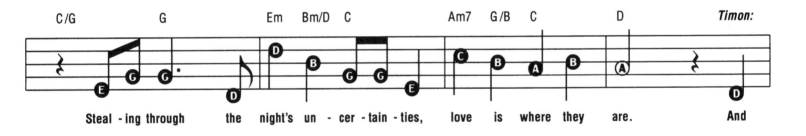

Steal - ing through the night's un - cer - tain - ties, love is where they are. And

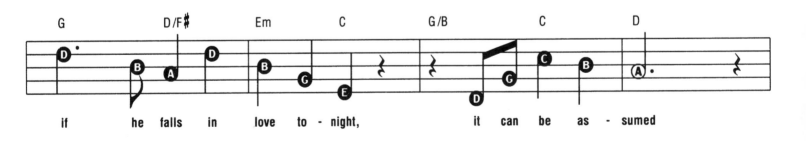

if he falls in love to - night, it can be as - sumed

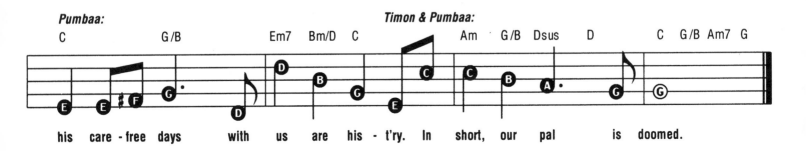

his care - free days with us are his - t'ry. In short, our pal is doomed.

Beauty And The Beast
from Walt Disney's BEAUTY AND THE BEAST

Lyrics by Howard Ashman
Music by Alan Menken

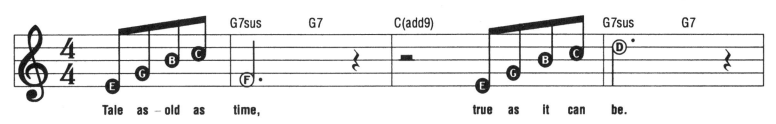

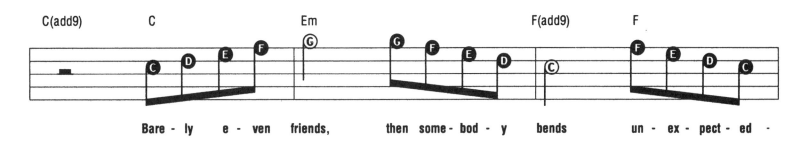

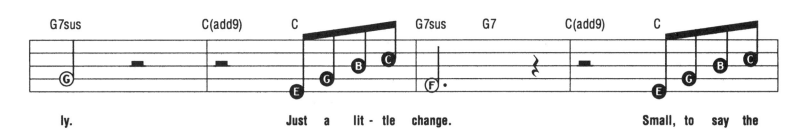

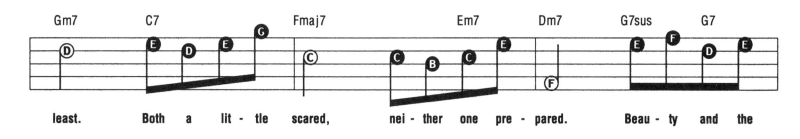

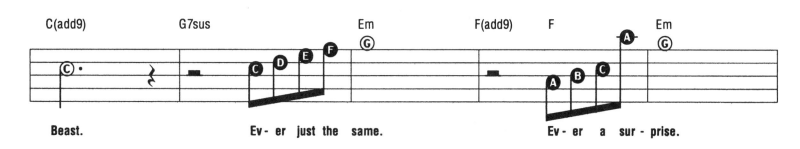

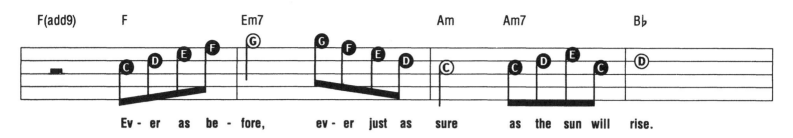

Ev - er as be - fore, ev - er just as sure as the sun will rise.

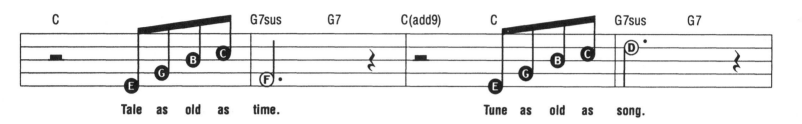

Tale as old as time. Tune as old as song.

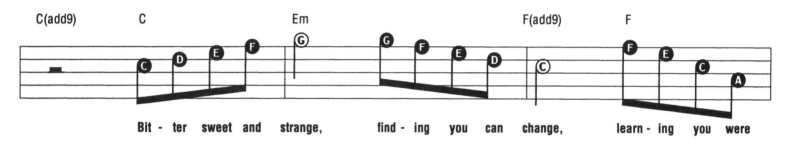

Bit - ter sweet and strange, find - ing you can change, learn - ing you were

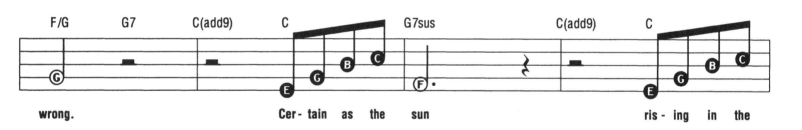

wrong. Cer - tain as the sun ris - ing in the

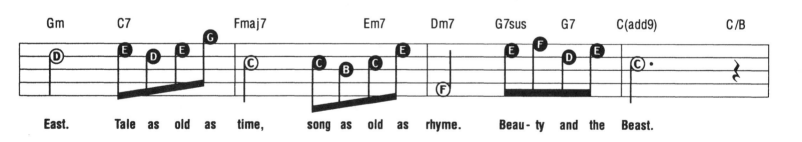

East. Tale as old as time, song as old as rhyme. Beau - ty and the Beast.

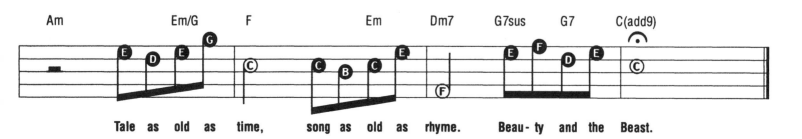

Tale as old as time, song as old as rhyme. Beau - ty and the Beast.

Reflection
from Walt Disney Pictures' MULAN

Music by Matthew Wilder
Lyrics by David Zippel

Under The Sea
from Walt Disney's THE LITTLE MERMAID

Lyrics by Howard Ashman
Music by Alan Menken

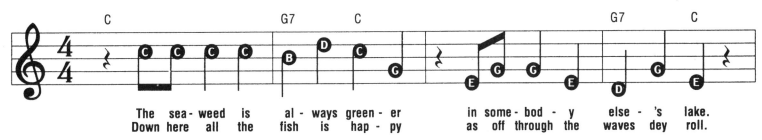

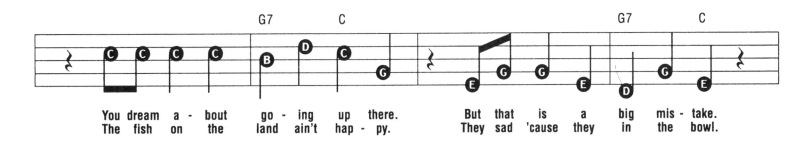

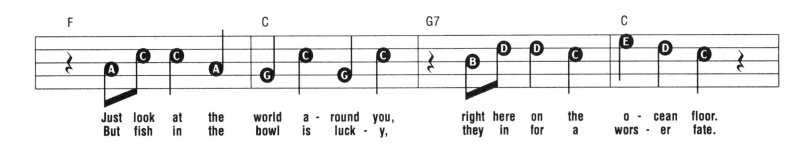

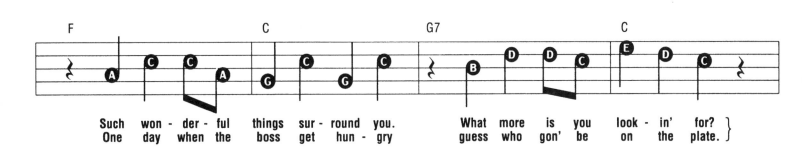

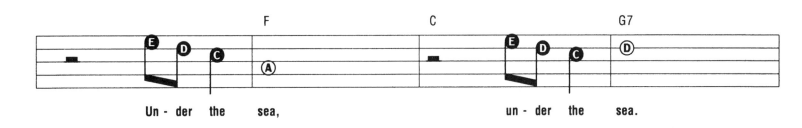

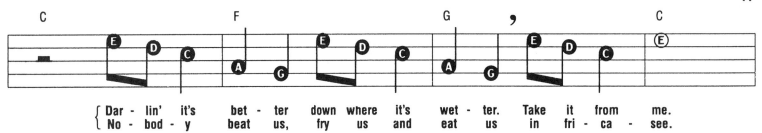

Dar - lin' it's bet - ter down where it's wet - ter. Take it from me.
No - bod - y beat us, fry us and eat us in fri - ca - see.

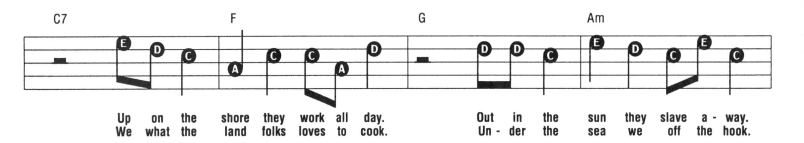

Up on the shore they work all day. Out in the sun they slave a - way.
We what the land folks loves to cook. Un - der the sea we off the hook.

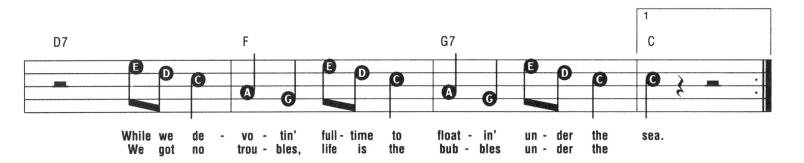

While we de - vo - tin' full - time to float - in' un - der the sea.
We got no trou - bles, life is the bub - bles un - der the

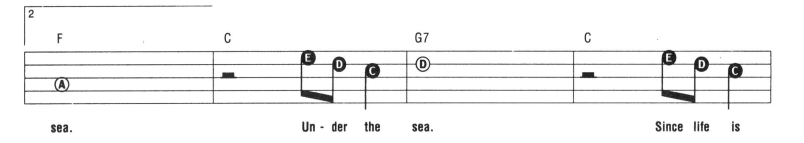

sea. Un - der the sea. Since life is

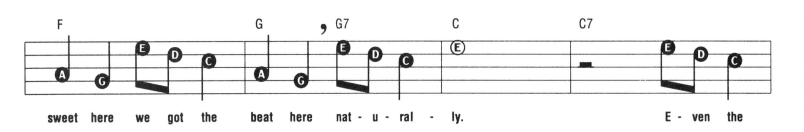

sweet here we got the beat here nat - u - ral - ly. E - ven the

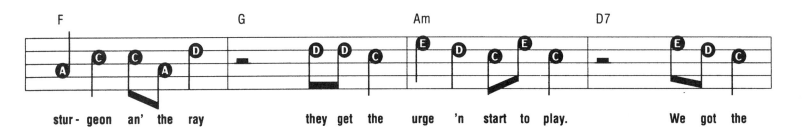

stur - geon an' the ray they get the urge 'n start to play. We got the

18

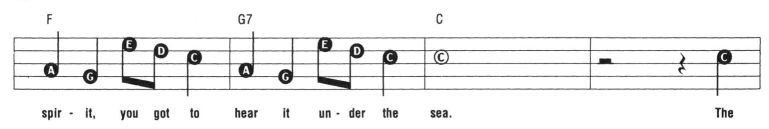

spir - it, you got to hear it un - der the sea. The

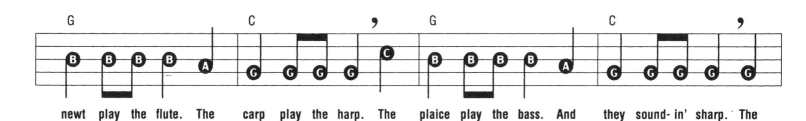

newt play the flute. The carp play the harp. The plaice play the bass. And they sound- in' sharp. The

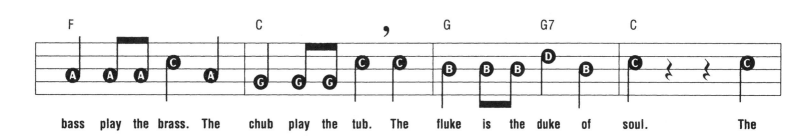

bass play the brass. The chub play the tub. The fluke is the duke of soul. The

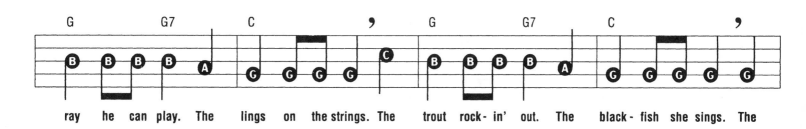

ray he can play. The lings on the strings. The trout rock- in' out. The black - fish she sings. The

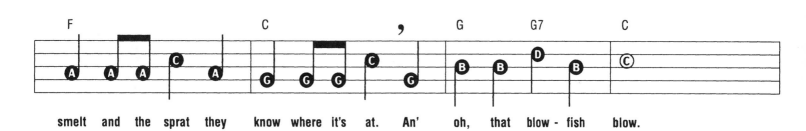

smelt and the sprat they know where it's at. An' oh, that blow - fish blow.

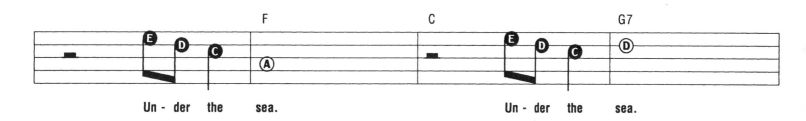

Un - der the sea. Un - der the sea.

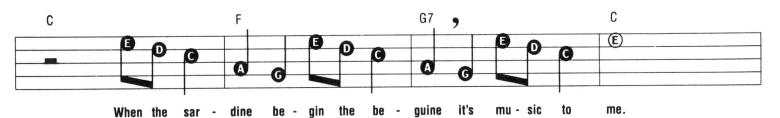

When the sar - dine be - gin the be - guine it's mu - sic to me.

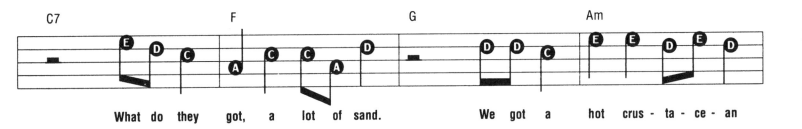

What do they got, a lot of sand. We got a hot crus - ta - ce - an

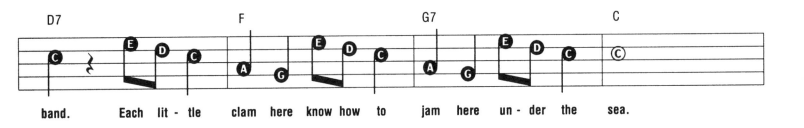

band. Each lit - tle clam here know how to jam here un - der the sea.

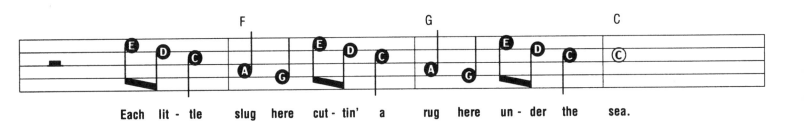

Each lit - tle slug here cut - tin' a rug here un - der the sea.

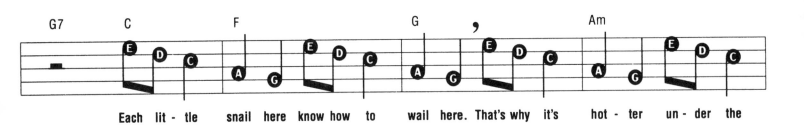

Each lit - tle snail here know how to wail here. That's why it's hot - ter un - der the

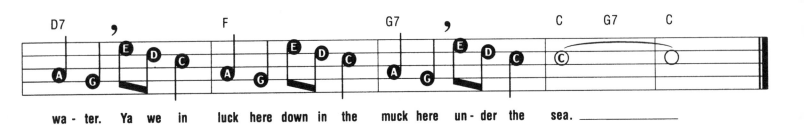

wa - ter. Ya we in luck here down in the muck here un - der the sea. _____

A Whole New World
from Walt Disney's ALADDIN

Music by Alan Menken
Lyrics by Tim Rice

Aladdin: I can show you the world,
I can o - pen your eyes

Jasmine: Un - be - lieve - a - ble sights

shin - ing, shim - mer - ing,
take you won - der by
in - de - scrib - a - ble

splen - did.
won - der
feel - ing.

Tell me prin - cess, now when did you last
O - ver, side - ways and un - der on a
Soar - ing, tum - bling free - wheel - ing through an

let your heart de - cide?
mag - ic car - pet
end - less dia - mond

ride. A whole new world _____
sky. A whole new world _____

You've Got A Friend In Me
from Walt Disney's TOY STORY

Music and Lyrics by
Randy Newman

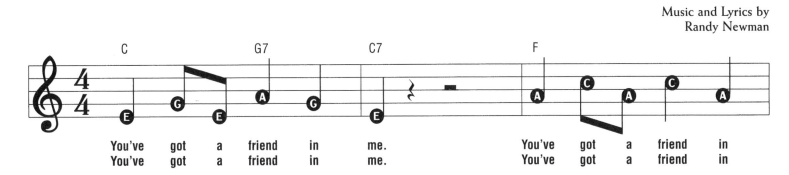

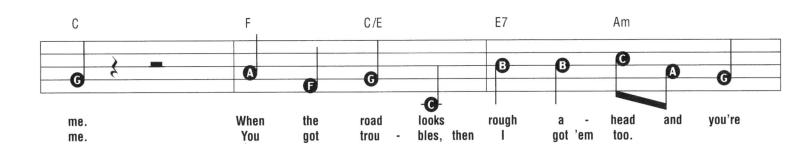

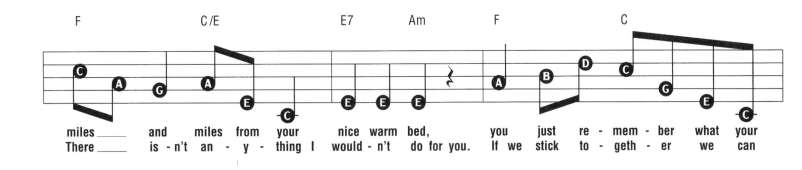

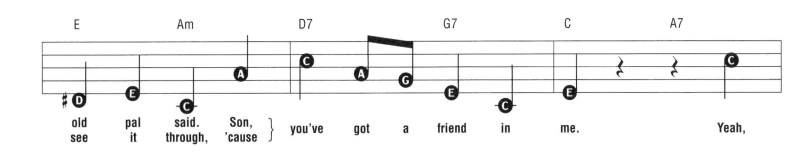

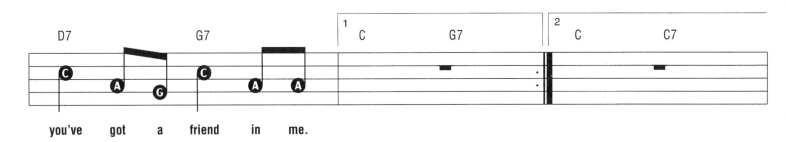

23

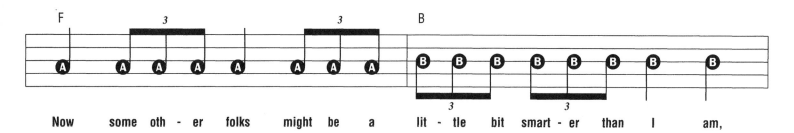

Now some oth - er folks might be a lit - tle bit smart - er than I am,

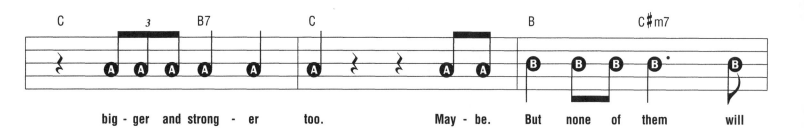

big - ger and strong - er too. May - be. But none of them will

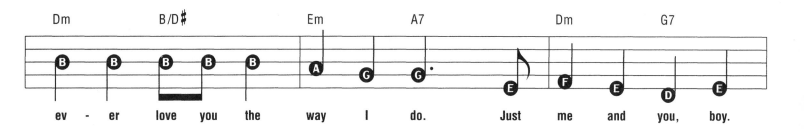

ev - er love you the way I do. Just me and you, boy.

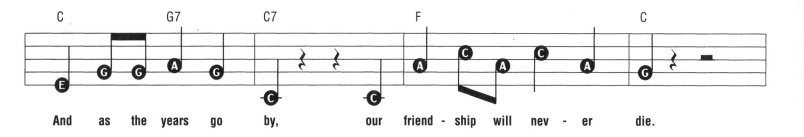

And as the years go by, our friend - ship will nev - er die.

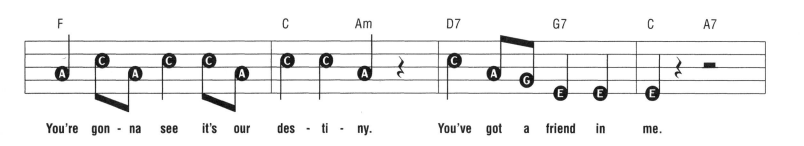

You're gon - na see it's our des - ti - ny. You've got a friend in me.

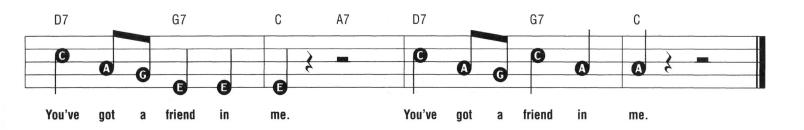

You've got a friend in me. You've got a friend in me.